WORLD ALMANAC®

Library of
American
GOVERNMENT

The
CABINET
AND FEDERAL AGENCIES

BY GEOFFREY M. HORN

WORLD ALMANAC® LIBRARY

Please visit our web site at: www.worldalmanaclibrary.com
For a free color catalog describing World Almanac® Library's list
of high-quality books and multimedia programs, call 1-800-848-2928 (USA)
or 1-800-387-3178 (Canada). World Almanac® Library's fax: (414) 332-3567.

Library of Congress Cataloging-in-Publication Data

Horn, Geoffrey M.
    The cabinet and federal agencies / by Geoffrey M. Horn.
        p. cm. — (World Almanac Library of American government)
    Includes bibliographical references and index.
    ISBN 0-8368-5476-4 (lib. bdg.)
    ISBN 0-8368-5481-0 (softcover)
    Contents: Making government work — What the Constitution says — Serving human needs —Using and preserving natural
resources — Managing the economy — Extending influence overseas — Law enforcement and homeland security.
    1. Administrative agencies—United States—Juvenile literature. 2. Executive departments—United States—Juvenile
literature. [1. Administrative agencies. 2. Executive departments. 3. United States—Politics and government.] I. Title.
II. Series.
JK421.H67   2003
351.73—dc21   2003053541

First published in 2004 by
World Almanac® Library
330 West Olive Street, Suite 100
Milwaukee, WI 53212 USA

Copyright © 2004 by World Almanac® Library.

Project editor: Alan Wachtel
Project manager: Jonny Brown
Cover design and layout: Melissa Valuch
Photo research: Diane Laska-Swanke
Indexer: Walter Kronenberg
Production: Beth Meinholz

Photo credits: © AP/Wide World Photos: 7 top, 9, 10, 14 top, 23, 24 bottom, 25, 30, 35, 38; © Annie Griffiths
Belt/CORBIS: 4 right; © Bettmann/CORBIS: 4 left, 17, 31; © Anna Clopet/CORBIS: 36 top; Courtesy National
Archives and Records Administration: cover (background), title page; © Ed Eckstein/CORBIS: 21 top; © Jon
Feingersh/CORBIS: 29; © Raymond Gehman/CORBIS: 39; © Sandy Huffaker/Getty Images: 21 bottom; © Hulton
Archive/Getty Images: 11, 12, 33, 34 bottom; © Shelly Katz/Getty Images: 37; © Julie Lemberger/CORBIS: 16;
© James Leynse/CORBIS SABA: 14 bottom; © David McNew/Getty Images: 19; NASA: 8; © North Wind Picture
Archives: cover (main); © Nova Development Corporation: 20; © Spencer Platt/Getty Images: 24 top; © Roger
Ressmeyer/CORBIS: 7 bottom; © Ariel Skelley/CORBIS: 15; © Mike Theiler/Getty Images: 34 top; © Robert
Trippett/Getty Images: 6; U.S. Census Bureau: 27; © U.S. Customs/Getty Images: 36 bottom; © U.S. Fish and
Wildlife Service/Getty Images: 18; Melissa Valuch/© World Almanac® Library, 2004: 5, 28; © Alex Wong/Getty
Images: 32

Printed in the United States of America

1 2 3 4 5 6 7 8 9 0 07 06 05 01 03

About the Author

GEOFFREY M. HORN is a freelance writer and editor with a lifelong interest in politics and the
arts. He is the author of books for young people and adults, and has contributed hundreds of articles to
encyclopedias and other reference books, including *The World Almanac*. He lives in southwestern Virginia,
in the foothills of the Blue Ridge Mountains, with his wife, four cats (at last count), and one rambunctious
collie. He dedicates this book to Frank and Izaline Davidson and to the memory of Phil Horn.

TABLE OF CONTENTS

Words that
appear in the
glossary
are printed in
boldface type
the first time
they occur in
the text.

Chapter One

MAKING GOVERNMENT WORK

If the United States government were a business, it would be the largest company in the history of the world. It provides employment for millions of people and owns over 430,000 buildings, along with more than one-fourth of the entire land area of the United States. The U.S. government has sent astronauts to the moon, transported huge armies halfway around the globe, and provided more than $500 billion in aid to other countries.

To keep this huge enterprise going, it takes money—lots of money. The **federal government** spends over $2 trillion every year. How much money is that? Roughly speaking, $2 trillion is enough to give a ten-dollar bill to every human being who ever lived and still have hundreds of billions of dollars left over. If you started spending $2 trillion at a rate of one thousand dollars a minute, it would take you about four thousand years to spend it all—and that's only if you earned no interest on any of your savings!

▼ Federal government employees deliver mail, inspect meat-processing plants, and perform many other important jobs.

Most years, the federal government spends more than it takes in. In fact, the federal government now owes more than $6 trillion in debt. That debt burden totals more than $20,000 for every American alive today.

FEDERAL GOVERNMENT INCOME, SPENDING, AND DEBT
(IN BILLIONS OF DOLLARS)

	Income	Spending	Surplus or Deficit (-)	Total Federal Debt
1960	92.5	92.2	0.3	290.5
1965	116.8	118.2	-1.4	322.3
1970	192.8	195.6	-2.8	380.9
1975	279.1	332.3	-53.2	541.9
1980	517.1	590.9	-73.8	909.1
1985	734.1	946.4	-212.3	1,817.5
1990	1,032.0	1,253.2	-221.2	3,206.6
1995	1,351.8	1,515.8	-164.0	4,921.0
2000	2,025.2	1,788.8	236.4	5,629.0
2001	1,991.0	1,863.9	127.1	5,770.3
2002 (est.)	1,946.1	2,052.3	-106.2	6,137.1

SOURCE: U.S. Office of Management and Budget

WHO WORKS FOR THE FEDERAL GOVERNMENT?

Today, of the 2,700,000 **civilians** who work for the federal government, fewer than six hundred are actually elected to their jobs. These elected officials include the president and vice president, the one hundred members of the Senate, and the 435 voting members of the House of Representatives. Another 6,500 or so employees are chosen by the president or approved by his staff. These government employees are known as political appointees.

Civilian federal employees who are not elected officials or political appointees are known as career civil servants. Their job is to carry out the policies set by the president, Congress, and the political appointees. These career civil servants are the people who actually collect taxes, deliver the mail, check the safety of

When the Nation Was Young

Things were different in George Washington's day. During the first president's first term (1789–1793), the entire federal government ran on a budget of less than $5 million a year. Today, $5 million would not be enough to keep the government running for two minutes!

the nation's food supply, and make sure the nation's soldiers get the equipment they need.

Although the total of 2,700,000 federal civilian jobs may seem very large, they make up only a small fraction of the jobs actually funded by federal money. Funds from the federal government also pay the salaries of the nearly 1,400,000 members of the armed forces. In addition, federal dollars fund jobs for millions of workers through contracts between private employers and the federal government.

THE EXECUTIVE BRANCH

Most federal employees work for the **executive branch**— the part of the federal government that is headed by the president. The executive branch carries out the laws passed by Congress. In general, the more laws Congress passes, the more departments and agencies the executive branch needs to carry them out. Like the White House, most of these departments and agencies are located in and around Washington, D.C., the nation's capital.

The executive branch includes the cabinet, the Executive Office of the President, and many independent agencies.

▼ President George W. Bush addresses the media after meeting at the White House with cabinet members and other top officials.

• **Cabinet:** The president's cabinet consists of the heads of the fifteen major government departments. These are, in alphabetical order, the departments of Agriculture, Commerce, Defense, Education, Energy, Health and Human Services, Homeland Security, Housing and Urban Development, Interior, Justice, Labor, State, Transportation, Treasury, and Veterans Affairs. The heads of all these departments are called secretaries except for the top official of the Justice Department, who holds the title of **attorney general**.

The president may also allow other members of the executive branch to attend cabinet meetings and hold cabinet rank.

• **Executive Office of the President:** The Executive Office of the President helps the president develop and carry out his policies and programs. It includes about a dozen White House offices and agencies. Two of the most important parts of the Executive Office of the President are the National Security Council, which advises the president on foreign policy, and the Office of Management and Budget, which puts together the budget the president submits to Congress each year.

• **Independent Agencies:** The executive branch has more than four dozen independent agencies, commissions, foundations, and corporations. One of these bodies, the U.S. Postal Service, has more than 800,000 employees— the largest civilian work force of any federal government agency. Other well known organizations in this group include the Central Intelligence Agency (CIA), the Environmental Protection Agency (EPA), and the Social Security Administration. The independent agencies are called independent because they do not belong to the Executive Office of the President or to any of the fifteen cabinet departments. Some of these

◀ Every president depends on White House staff members to help him govern. This 1993 photo shows aides to President Bill Clinton (left) announcing staff changes in the White House Communications Office. Key figures in the shakeup were George Stephanopoulos (at microphone) and David Gergen (third from right).

▼ An operations center at the Central Intelligence Agency, as it looked in 1990.

independent agencies also operate under special laws that limit the ability of the president or Congress to control their activities.

The Sky's No Limit

NASA is a name known round the world—and perhaps on other worlds as well. The initials stand for National Aeronautics and Space Administration, the independent agency that runs the space program of the U.S. government.

NASA was founded at a time when the United States and the Soviet Union were rival superpowers. On October 4, 1957, the Soviet Union launched the first artificial satellite, Sputnik, into Earth's orbit. Concerned that the United States might be losing the "space race," President Dwight Eisenhower proposed the creation of NASA in 1958.

In 1961, in a speech to Congress, President John F. Kennedy issued this exciting challenge:

I believe that this nation should commit itself to achieving the goal, before this decade is out, of landing a man on the moon and returning him safely to the earth. No single space project in this period will be more impressive to mankind, or more important for the long-range exploration of space; and none will be so difficult or expensive to accomplish.

Remarkably, only eight years later, NASA accomplished this goal with the Apollo 11 mission. NASA spacecraft have also explored Mars, approached Jupiter and Saturn, and sent back startling photographs from the outer reaches of the solar system.

▲ The space shuttle *Discovery* blasts off from the Kennedy Space Center.

Many of NASA's projects are closely covered by the media, so when a mission ends in disaster, the entire world knows about it right away. A terrible fire during a ground test of the Apollo spacecraft killed three crew members in 1967. The tragic losses of two space shuttles—*Challenger* in 1986 and *Columbia* in 2003—cost the lives of a total of fourteen astronauts.

Today, NASA's work is driven not by superpower rivalry but by a quest to unlock some of the deepest mysteries of the universe. With the collapse of the Soviet Union, Russia has taken over what remains of the Soviet space program. NASA is working together with the Russian, European, Japanese, and Canadian space agencies to build and operate the International Space Station.

Chapter Two

WHAT THE CONSTITUTION SAYS

The Constitution does not say very much about how the executive branch should be organized. The word "cabinet," for example, does not appear anywhere in the Constitution.

Article II, Section 2 states that the president "may require the Opinion in writing, of the principal Officer in each of the executive Departments, upon any subject relating to the Duties of their respective Offices." The Constitution does not say, however, how many departments should be created, what their names and functions should be, how many employees they may hire, or how much money they may spend. Those decisions are left to the president and Congress.

▲ Participating in this 1983 swearing-in ceremony were, from left to right: President Ronald Reagan; Elizabeth Hanford Dole, the new secretary of transportation; her mother, Mary Hanford; Supreme Court Justice Sandra Day O'Connor; and Dole's husband, U.S. Senator Bob Dole of Kansas.

POWER OF APPOINTMENT

Two groups of executive branch employees are described in Article II, Section 2. Employees in the first group are appointed by the president but must be confirmed by a majority of the Senate. This group includes the top-ranking members of the various government departments: cabinet secretaries, deputy secretaries, undersecretaries, and assistant secretaries. Also among this first group are the heads of the independent agencies, such as NASA, and the more than one hundred and eighty **ambassadors** who represent the U.S. government in foreign countries.

Cabinet "Firsts"

The first cabinet department established by the U.S. Congress was the Department of Foreign Affairs, on July 27, 1789. On September 15, it was renamed the Department of State, the name it still holds today.

Like the great majority of other top officials of the United States, most cabinet heads have been white, Protestant males. The first female member of the cabinet was Frances Perkins, who became secretary of labor in 1933. The cabinet's first African-American was Robert C. Weaver, who became secretary of housing and urban development in 1966.

The second group consists of certain lower-ranking officials and members of the president's own staff. Members of this second group are chosen by the president, presidential staff members, or department heads, but they do not require confirmation by the Senate.

Most of the president's choices to head the cabinet departments and executive agencies sail through the Senate with little trouble. Once in a while, however, a nominee faces serious opposition. In late December 2000, for example, President-elect George W. Bush named John Ashcroft, a **conservative** Republican, to become attorney general. Many Democrats opposed the nomination. They claimed that Ashcroft—who was against gun control and abortion, and took a go-slow approach to civil rights—was a poor choice to head the Justice Department, where he would need to enforce many laws he personally disliked.

▼ John Ashcroft was confirmed as attorney general after a tough Senate battle in 2001. The photo shows him in Salt Lake City, Utah, a year later, discussing security plans for the Winter Olympics.

Ashcroft responded by saying he understood that being attorney general meant "enforcing the laws as they are written, not enforcing my personal preferences." At the beginning of February 2001, the Senate confirmed him by a vote of fifty-eight to forty-two. All forty-two votes against him came from Democrats.

The Spoils System

Nearly all winning political candidates try to use their appointment power to reward their most loyal supporters. This is known as political patronage, or the "spoils system."

The spoils system dominated American politics for much of the nineteenth century, when most government job holders were political appointees. By the early 1880s, however, it became clear that many government employees were incompetent or dishonest. These hacks had bought their jobs through money or party service.

When James Garfield became president in 1881 he found job seekers circling around him "like vultures for a wounded bison." Four months after he took office, he was shot by a man who was angry because Garfield had refused to give him a government job. After Garfield died, the new president, Chester Alan Arthur, became a champion of government reform.

In 1883, Congress moved to clean up government service by passing the Pendleton Act. This law set up the Civil Service Commission to replace the spoils system with a system based on merit. Today, only about one of every four hundred government job holders is a political appointee. The Civil Service Commission was replaced in 1978 by the Office of Personnel Management, an independent agency. All these changes have helped make the federal government more effective in supplying services to people who really need them.

◀ The murder of President James Garfield by a disappointed job seeker spurred the movement for civil service reform. Here, Garfield staggers after being shot in the back, while an angry crowd (left) subdues his attacker.

POWER OF REMOVAL

Although the Constitution grants to the president the power to appoint top government officials, it is much less clear on the question of who has the power to remove them. Article II, Section 4 says that Congress may use the

impeachment process to remove "the President, the Vice President and all civil Officers of the United States." Would the president also need the consent of Congress in order to fire a cabinet member or some other high-ranking federal employee?

The **framers** of the Constitution disagreed on this question. The dispute led to a crisis after the **Civil War**, when Congress passed the Tenure of Office Act. This 1867 law required the president to seek Senate approval before removing any federal employee whom the Senate had confirmed. The measure was aimed at preventing President Andrew Johnson, who took a lenient attitude toward the South, from firing any high official who favored the tougher policy that Congress promoted.

Early in 1868, President Johnson violated the Tenure of Office Act by firing Secretary of War Edwin M. Stanton. Congress reacted angrily and launched impeachment proceedings against Johnson. The president was impeached by the House in February, but the Senate failed by one vote to convict him in May.

The Tenure of Office Act was repealed in 1887, but disputes over the power to hire and fire have flared up since that time. In 1993, for example, President Bill Clinton was criticized for firing the entire staff of the White House Travel Office. Critics said the workers were fired because the president and First Lady Hillary Rodham Clinton wanted to help some friends and supporters who were in the travel business.

▼ **The verdict in the 1868 impeachment trial of Andrew Johnson shows thirty-five senators voting guilty and nineteen voting not guilty. The number voting for conviction fell one short of the two-thirds majority needed to remove Johnson from office.**

SERVING HUMAN NEEDS

Chapter Three

The federal government has been involved in protecting the nation's health since the first Marine Hospital was established to care for sailors in 1798. Another important step was taken in 1906 with the passage of the Food and Drug Act, intended to safeguard the country's supply of food and medicines. Many social welfare programs were started in the 1930s as part of President Franklin D. Roosevelt's New Deal.

Government activities that support health, education, and welfare were gathered together in the new Federal Security Agency in 1939. The agency was renamed the Department of Health, Education, and Welfare (HEW) and made part of the cabinet in 1953. HEW became the Department of Health and Human Services (HHS) in 1979, when education was given its own cabinet department.

DEPARTMENT OF HEALTH AND HUMAN SERVICES

The Department of Health and Human Services has more than 60,000 employees and spends over $500 billion each year. Most of that money is spent by the Centers for Medicare and Medicaid Services on two programs: Medicare, which provides health insurance for people who are at least sixty-five years old, and Medicaid, which finances health care for people with low incomes. This agency also operates the State Children's Health Insurance Program and regulates much of the testing done by the nearly 158,000 medical laboratories throughout the United States.

Other important divisions of the Department of Health and Human Services include:

• **Centers for Disease Control and Prevention (CDC):** The CDC, which has its headquarters in Atlanta, Georgia,

▲ Elizabeth Hunsperger, a microbiologist, studies the West Nile virus at a CDC laboratory. The virus, which is spread by mosquitoes, can cause serious illness.

takes a frontline role in dealing with immediate health threats. For example, when a new disease known as SARS—severe acute respiratory syndrome—spread from China to the United States, the CDC sprang into action, warning the public and the medical profession. Researchers for the CDC also began working on ways to stop the spread of SARS.

• **Food and Drug Administration (FDA):** No new drug or medical device can be marketed in the United States without FDA approval. The FDA also monitors the safety of the nation's blood supply and makes sure that foods are processed in ways that do not create health hazards. At times, the FDA issues public warnings about items that may be dangerous. In early 2003, for example, the agency warned that people who used ephedra, a substance found in certain weight-loss products, risked heart attacks, seizures, and death.

• **National Institutes of Health (NIH):** The NIH, which began as a one-room laboratory in 1887, now embraces more than two dozen separate research divisions. Separate institutes deal with early childhood diseases, cancer, heart disease, alcohol and drug abuse, environmental health problems, and mental disorders, among many other important health issues.

▼ By law, every cigarette pack must carry a health warning from the U.S. surgeon general. Warnings must also appear in cigarette advertisements.

• **Office of the Surgeon General:** The surgeon general is a leading spokesman on public health matters. By law, packs of cigarettes or cigars sold in the United States must carry a warning from the surgeon general about the dangers of smoking.

SOCIAL SECURITY ADMINISTRATION

About one of every six Americans receives money from Social Security, the nation's largest social insurance program. The program was begun in 1935, while the country was in a severe economic depression. The Social Security Administration became an independent agency in the mid-1990s.

Today, the Social Security Administration spends more money each year than any other federal government department or agency. The main Social Security program—officially known as Old-age, Survivors, and Disability Insurance—provides monthly payments to people who have retired or who are disabled. Benefits are also paid to the husbands or wives and children of disabled workers or of insured workers who have died.

▼ **The Social Security system has expanded to match the changing needs and growing number of elderly Americans.**

The system is financed through taxes on workers, employers, and the self-employed. In 1950, fewer than 3.5 million people received money from the program, and the average payment was less

A Promise Kept

Some people worry that because many millions of workers are approaching retirement age, the Social Security system may not have enough money to pay for them all. Although some changes will need to be made, political support for the program remains as strong as ever.

Every president since Franklin D. Roosevelt has expressed the nation's commitment to Social Security. In 1990, President George H. W. Bush said:

To every American out there on Social Security, to every American supporting that system today, and to everyone counting on it when they retire, we made a promise to you, and we are going to keep it.

than $300 a year. Fifty years later, more than 45 million people received monthly Social Security checks, and the average annual benefit totaled almost $9,000.

DEPARTMENT OF EDUCATION

About ninety cents of every dollar spent on education comes from the state governments, local communities, and private sources. The remaining ten cents comes from the federal government. Because the United States has a very strong tradition of state and local control in public schooling, the Department of Education speaks with a less powerful voice than similar agencies in other countries.

Nevertheless, the federal department remains a dependable source of aid for schools throughout the United States. It spends more than $60 billion a year to support all levels

Funds for the Arts

Although tiny by comparison with other government programs, federal arts funding programs can make a huge difference to struggling local arts groups. The National Endowment for the Arts, an independent agency, provides support for traditional and modern works in dance, music, theater, and other art forms. Another independent agency, the National Endowment for the Humanities, aids the research and educational projects of museums, libraries, colleges, cultural institutions, and scholars.

▲ Money from the federal government helps dance companies and other arts groups pay their bills.

of education, some of which takes the form of financial aid for college students. This support allows many students to attend college who could not otherwise afford to do so.

Not all of the federal money spent on schools comes from the Department of Education. For example, Head Start, a program that helps very young children from low-income families, is managed by the Department of Health and Human Services.

DEPARTMENT OF HOUSING AND URBAN DEVELOPMENT

The mission of the Department of Housing and Urban Development (HUD) is to ensure that every American has a "decent, safe, and sanitary home and suitable living environment." HUD aims to enforce fair housing laws, encourage home ownership, revive declining neighborhoods, assist low-income families, and help the homeless.

HUD began with high hopes in 1965, when the cabinet department was created as part of President Lyndon Johnson's Great Society program. The idea behind HUD was to pump new life into America's inner cities, many of which were troubled by poverty, racism, crime, and drugs.

Despite HUD's many accomplishments, the department has had a troubled history. Funds for urban housing dwindled during most of the 1980s, when HUD was poorly managed and plagued with scandals. HUD's record has improved since then, but the department has still not fulfilled its early promise.

▽ **Built in the early 1950s, the Pruitt-Igoe housing project in St. Louis, Missouri, soon became a crime-ridden slum; the apartment buildings were demolished in the early 1970s. Many U.S. cities still face a shortage of safe, affordable housing.**

Chapter Four

USING AND PRESERVING NATURAL RESOURCES

▲ **The oil-rich Arctic National Wildlife Refuge poses difficult policy choices. Americans must decide whether they want to expand the nation's energy supply or preserve this Alaskan region as an unspoiled wilderness.**

The federal government oversees the development and protection of the nation's water, wetlands, farms, forests, minerals, and other natural resources. Parts of the executive branch that deal with resource management and preservation include the Environmental Protection Agency and the departments of Agriculture, Interior, and Energy.

DEPARTMENT OF AGRICULTURE

Making sure that Americans have a plentiful supply of nutritious food is the responsibility of the U.S. Department of Agriculture (USDA). The USDA tries to ensure that farmers can earn enough from the sales of crops and live-stock products to keep their farms going. In addition, the USDA helps to promote the sale of U.S. farm products over-seas. American farm exports earn more than $50 billion a year and supply much of the world's demand for corn, soy-beans, wheat, cotton, rice, and meat products.

Within the United States, the USDA assists consumers as well as producers of farm products. The department's Food and Nutrition Service provides more than $30 billion in aid each year to low-income families. These efforts include the Food Stamp Program, which each month helps millions of low-income families to obtain groceries; the Women, Infants and Children (WIC) Program, which assists women who are pregnant or breastfeeding, as well as other families with very young children; and the National School Lunch and School Breakfast programs.

▲ **The Fulton Hot Shots of the U.S. Forest Service battle a blaze near Pine Valley, California.**

The USDA includes within it the Forest Service, which manages the nation's 155 national forests and twenty national grasslands. In the national forests under its control, the Forest Service must balance competing demands on the nation's timber resources; timber companies want to use the forests for logging, vacationers want to use the forests for hiking and camping, and environmentalists want to preserve the forests as wildlife habitats. The Forest Service also has the task of making sure that wildfires— a natural part of the life cycle of every wilderness—do not get out of control and threaten populated areas.

DEPARTMENT OF THE INTERIOR

Another cabinet department that helps to oversee the land resources of the United States is the Department of the Interior. Among its major divisions are the:

• **Bureau of Land Management:** This bureau manages about one-eighth of the nation's land area, mostly in a

▲ **The Statue of Liberty and many other famous U.S. landmarks are managed by the National Park Service.**

dozen western states. In the particular areas under its control, the bureau decides which lands will be used for cattle grazing, logging, mining, or tourism, and which will be preserved as wilderness.

• **National Park Service (NPS):** The NPS manages more than 300 separate areas. These include natural treasures like the Grand Canyon and Yellowstone; national symbols like the Statue of Liberty, the Lincoln Memorial, and Mount Rushmore; and an extraordinary variety of national monuments, preserves, historic and battlefield sites, scenic trails, and recreation areas.

• **Fish and Wildlife Service:** The Fish and Wildlife Service manages 540 national wildlife refuges. It also maintains the list of **endangered species** in the United States. As of 2003, a total of 986 species were listed as endangered. Of these, 388 were animals and 598 were plants. Some of these species will disappear, but federal officials are trying hard to save as many as possible. In early 2003, for example, the Fish and Wildlife Service claimed victory in helping the gray wolf survive in two regions, the western Great Lakes states and the northern Rocky Mountains.

• **Bureau of Indian Affairs:** This bureau conducts relations between the U.S. government and the about 1.5 million Native Americans (including American Indians and Alaska Natives) who belong to more than 560 federally recognized tribes. The bureau was founded as part of the War Department in 1824; it was moved to the Department of the Interior when that department was established twenty-five years later.

For Whose Benefit?

Under a program that began in 1887, the Bureau of Indian Affairs is supposed to manage more than 55 million acres (over 22 million hectares) of Indian lands for the benefit of Native Americans. The program allows private firms to lease the grazing, mining, and timber rights from the government, which then gives the money to the Indians who actually own the land. Many Native Americans, however, believe that the government and the private companies have worked together to cheat them out of tens of billions of dollars. A group of Native Americans filed a lawsuit against the Department of the Interior in 1996, and the issue is still very much in dispute.

⬛ Native Americans have long complained of low incomes and poor living conditions on U.S. reservations. This photograph was taken around 1970.

DEPARTMENT OF ENERGY

Americans have an apparently unquenchable thirst for energy. Farms, factories, hospitals, computers, SUVs—all these need energy to make them go. The United States is both the world's largest producer and the world's largest consumer of energy. Because the nation consumes so much more energy than it produces, it is also the world's largest energy importer. Much of that imported energy reaches the United States in the form of oil.

The Department of Energy was created in 1977, at the height of what was then called the "energy crisis." Federal officials were concerned about a worldwide rise in the price of oil. They believed that the nation's continued reliance on imported oil threatened the nation's security. They also worried that worldwide

▼ San Diego, California, is the site of this energy-efficient home, which uses rooftop solar panels to turn sunlight into electricity.

reserves of **fossil fuels** such as oil, coal, and natural gas—which nature had taken many millions of years to create—might begin to run out within a few decades. More recently, experts have warned that burning fossil fuels harms the environment by contributing to **global warming**.

Nuclear Watchdogs

In addition to its civilian work, the Department of Energy (DOE) has military obligations. The DOE oversees the nation's stockpile of nuclear weapons. It also works to make sure that nuclear weapons do not get into the hands of countries and groups that might use them against the United States.

The Nuclear Regulatory Commission, an independent agency, acts as a watchdog over the nation's civilian nuclear power plants.

The goals of the Department of Energy are:
- To increase domestic energy production, thereby reducing the country's dependence on energy imports;
- To promote energy conservation;
- To encourage Americans to use energy more efficiently;
- To foster the use of renewable energy sources, such as solar, wind, and water power.

Many buildings, factories, and home appliances are much more energy efficient than they were several decades ago. In other respects, however, progress toward the country's energy goals has been disappointing. For example, the nation relies more on imported oil today than it did in the 1970s. Some Americans hope to deal with this problem by drilling for more oil in the United States—especially in the Alaskan wilderness. Opponents of Alaskan drilling argue that this would harm the Arctic environment. They favor further conservation measures and the use of renewable energy sources, which would also reduce the threat of global warming.

ENVIRONMENTAL PROTECTION AGENCY

Making the nation a cleaner and healthier place to live is the prime job of the Environmental Protection Agency (EPA). Because of the EPA and the laws it enforces, the nation's air and water are less polluted today than they were when the agency was founded in 1970. The EPA has also helped to clean up toxic waste dumps, some of them more than one hundred years old. Wherever possible, the EPA tries to make the company that used the land as a dumping ground pay for the cost of the toxic waste cleanup.

Views about the EPA have varied over the years. In a speech in 1982, President Ronald Reagan expressed the irritation felt by some Americans when environmental laws limit what businesses and towns can do.

> *If the federal government had been around when the Creator was putting His hand to this state, Indiana wouldn't be here. It'd still be waiting for an environmental impact statement.*

The following remarks by Christine Todd Whitman, who headed the EPA from 2001 to 2003, reflect a more balanced approach:

> *In the short history of the agency . . . the EPA has helped underscore the universal agreement that our natural resources are valuable, not just for economic prosperity but for sustained quality of life. No longer do we debate whether we need to act to protect the environment. Rather we discuss how we can keep America green while keeping our economy growing.*

▼ EPA chief Christine Todd Whitman chats with a biology student at Virginia's College of William & Mary in 2002.

Chapter Five

MANAGING THE ECONOMY

▲ Traders work the floor of the New York Stock Exchange, where private companies raise capital to help businesses and the economy grow.

▼ An employee at the Bureau of Engraving and Printing inspects sheets of freshly printed dollar bills.

The annual value of all goods and services produced in the United States exceeds $10 trillion—about five times the amount the federal government spends each year. The United States has a free economy, which means that the federal government generally does not interfere in business decisions. However, many federal departments and agencies try to ensure that the national economy performs in a way that is efficient, honest, and fair.

DEPARTMENT OF THE TREASURY

One of the first cabinet departments established in 1789 was the Department of the Treasury. Today, the department manages the finances of the federal government. It also designs and makes the coins and currency used throughout the United States.

• **U.S. Mint:** The Treasury began minting coins in the early 1790s, using a horse-drawn press in Philadelphia. The press delivered its first coin order—a total of 11,178 copper cents—in 1793. The U.S. Mint, a division of the Treasury Department, still produces coins in Philadelphia today, and modern coin presses also operate in Denver, Colorado; San Francisco, California; and West Point, New York. The Denver Mint alone can churn out more than 50 million coins each day.

A Matter of Principle

No one in recent decades has had more power over the economy of the United States than Alan Greenspan. In 1987, Greenspan became the head of the Federal Reserve System, also known as "the Fed." Created in 1913, this independent agency serves as the nation's central bank. Actions by the Fed influence whether consumer prices rise or fall. The Fed's decisions also affect how much people pay in interest on home mortgages and credit cards.

In 1999, Greenspan described what he thought was the key to success in life:

▲ **Alan Greenspan (left) traveled to Beijing in 1998 to advise Chinese leaders on money policy.**

Material success is . . . far more satisfying when it comes without exploiting others. The true measure of a career is to be able to be content, even proud, that you succeeded through your own endeavors without leaving a trail of casualties in your wake. . . . In my working life, I have found no greater satisfaction than achieving success through honest dealings and strict adherence to the view that for you to gain, those you deal with should gain as well. . . . And beyond the personal sense of satisfaction, having a reputation for fair dealing is a profoundly practical virtue. We call it "good will" in business and add it to our balance sheets.

• **Bureau of Engraving and Printing:** This bureau produces paper money on some two dozen special presses in Fort Worth, Texas, and Washington, D.C. Some 37 million bills with a total value of nearly $700 million are printed each day. About 95 percent of the new paper money replaces bills that are worn out or torn.

• **Internal Revenue Service:** About two of every three employees in the Treasury Department work for the Internal Revenue Service (IRS), the federal government's tax collection division. Each year the IRS handles more than 220 million tax returns filed by companies and individual taxpayers.

• **Bureau of the Public Debt:** This bureau manages the federal debt, which is now more than $6 trillion (see Chapter 1). When the government spends more than it collects in taxes, the bureau finds ways to keep the government running. One way the bureau raises money is through the sale of U.S. savings bonds.

DEPARTMENTS OF COMMERCE AND LABOR

A single Department of Commerce and Labor was established in 1903 to promote U.S. businesses and to find foreign markets for U.S.-made goods. Ten years later, the department was split in two.

Now, as then, the Department of Commerce seeks to promote the country's economic growth. Among its divisions are the Patent and Trademark Office, which protects the rights of inventors to profit from their discoveries; the National Oceanographic and Atmospheric Administration, which includes the National Weather Service; and the Bureau of the Census, which gathers an enormous variety of information about who Americans are, where they live, and what they do.

Since 1913, the Department of Labor's mission has been to promote the welfare of American workers. This department administers federal laws that protect employees' rights to safe and sanitary working conditions, a minimum hourly wage, overtime pay, income assistance if they lose their jobs, and pension benefit protection when they retire.

One of the Department of Labor's high-profile divisions is the Occupational Safety and Health Administration (OSHA), which seeks to cut work-related injuries and illnesses. The rules OSHA issues for things like hard hats, ladders, and safety harnesses are detailed and highly technical, but their goal is simple: to save lives. OSHA employees try to stop accidents before they happen by

Making Every American Count

Article I, Section 2 of the Constitution requires the United States to count its population every ten years. The census has come a long way since 1790, when 17 U.S. marshals and about 600 assistant marshals traveled for 18 months on wretched roads to count fewer than 4 million people. In 2010, census planners expect that 500,000 workers equipped with handheld computers will count a population somewhere around 300 million.

The Bureau of the Census is a division of the Department of Commerce. When not conducting the census, the bureau collects other data on the nation's population and economy. Public cooperation is necessary to make this information as accurate as possible, so that businesses and government officials can have good data on which to base their decisions.

▲ **To get an accurate picture of the U.S. population in 2000, census takers went door-to-door checking up on people who did not send in their census forms.**

inspecting and correcting dangerous job sites, but the agency lacks the funds it needs to hire enough inspectors.

OTHER DEPARTMENTS AND AGENCIES

In addition to the Federal Reserve System and the Treasury, Commerce, and Labor departments, many other parts of the federal government take a hand in guiding the United States economy. These other departments and agencies include:

• **Department of Transportation (DOT):** This cabinet department was established by Congress in 1966. It oversees the highways, rails, ships, aircraft, and urban mass transit systems that bring people to work, carry goods to market, and link Americans with each other and the world. Passenger rail transportation is managed by an independent agency, the National Railroad Passenger

Corporation, better known as Amtrak. Another independent agency, the National Transportation Safety Board, investigates airplane crashes and other transportation accidents.

• **Office of Management and Budget (OMB):** Part of the Executive Office of the President, the OMB prepares the president's detailed annual budget request to Congress. Congress has the final word, however, on how much money each cabinet department and executive agency receives.

• **Federal Trade Commission (FTC):** The FTC, an independent **regulatory agency** created in 1914, enforces laws against unfair trade practices. The FTC takes action against false or misleading advertising, labeling, and packaging. It also seeks to prevent companies from using unfair

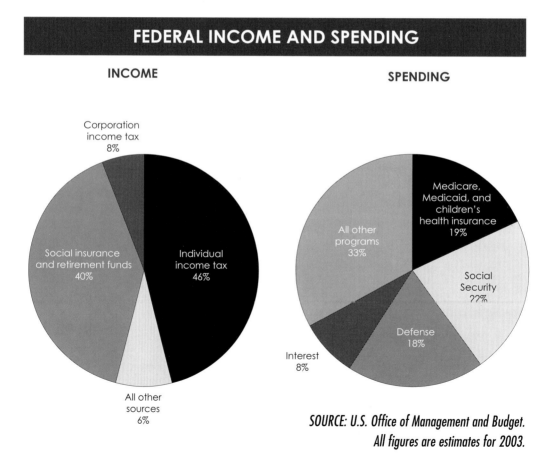

FEDERAL INCOME AND SPENDING

INCOME

Corporation
income tax
8%

Social insurance
and retirement funds
40%

Individual
income tax
46%

All other
sources
6%

SPENDING

Medicare,
Medicaid, and
children's
health insurance
19%

All other
programs
33%

Social
Security
22%

Defense
18%

Interest
8%

SOURCE: U.S. Office of Management and Budget.
All figures are estimates for 2003.

tactics to thwart competition or cheat consumers. Recently the FTC has been working on ways to reduce spam, or junk e-mail.

• **Federal Communications Commission (FCC):** Established in 1934, the FCC is an independent agency that regulates telecommunications in the United States. It oversees the radio, television, telephone, satellite, and cable communications industries.

• **Consumer Product Safety Commission (CPSC):** The CPSC is an independent regulatory agency created by Congress in 1972. It protects the public by trying to keep hazardous products off the market. For example, the CPSC has ordered the recall of bicycle helmets that failed to meet safety standards.

▼ **Bike helmet quality is a big concern at the federal Consumer Product Safety Commission. Riders wearing improperly made helmets could suffer serious head injuries in a fall.**

When Regulation Fails

Business leaders sometimes complain that federal laws, rules, and paperwork place an unfair burden on American companies. There is some truth to these complaints. But it is equally true that without alert, active, and honest federal regulators, people can be hurt in many ways.

The Securities and Exchange Commission (SEC) was created as an independent agency in 1934, to prevent some of the abuses that led to a stock market crash five years earlier. The job of the SEC is to make sure that people who buy stocks can get accurate and complete information about the companies in which they invest.

During the late 1990s, companies such as Enron and WorldCom attracted investors by putting out false information about how well they were doing. Government officials and others who were supposed to make sure these companies were giving accurate information did not warn investors in time. As a result, when these companies collapsed, investors lost billions of dollars, and the entire economy suffered.

Chapter Six

EXTENDING INFLUENCE OVERSEAS

▲ An F/A-18 *Hornet* all-weather fighter and attack aircraft takes off from the deck of the aircraft carrier USS *Kitty Hawk* during Operation Iraqi Freedom. The war, launched in March 2003 by the U.S. and its allies, toppled the government of Iraqi dictator Saddam Hussein.

The United States engages with the world in many ways. Each year American firms export over $1 trillion in goods and services to other countries, and they import even larger amounts in return. American pop music, films, fashions, and technology have worldwide impact.

United States embassies and consulates represent the nation's interests in nearly every world capital. Most countries have at least a handful of U.S. troops, who give military advice to the host country or provide security for Americans living there. More than 160,000 Americans have served as volunteers in the Peace Corps, helping over 130 countries improve their schools, farms, medical care, and other basic services.

DEPARTMENT OF STATE

Because so many people, with so many different agendas, represent the United States overseas, conducting the nation's foreign affairs can get very complicated. The main burden of making and carrying out U.S. foreign policy falls on the State Department, which is headed by the secretary of state. Many distinguished Americans have served as secretary of state, including four of the nation's first six presidents—Thomas Jefferson, James Madison, James Monroe, and John Quincy Adams. The first woman to head the State Department was Madeleine Korbel Albright, who served from 1997 to 2001. Colin Powell, who took office in 2001, is

The Marshall Plan

For more than forty years, George C. Marshall (1880–1959) was a professional soldier, and he was one of the greatest military commanders in U.S. history. In early 1947, President Harry S. Truman chose him as secretary of state. That June, Marshall gave an extraordinary speech in which he explained why the United States needed to help Germany and other European countries recover from the devastation of **World War II**.

▲ George C. Marshall as he appeared in 1951, after he left the State Department and was serving as secretary of defense.

The truth of the matter is that Europe's requirements for the next three or four years of foreign food and other essential products—principally from America—are so much greater than her present ability to pay that she must have substantial additional help or face economic, social, and political deterioration of a very grave character. The remedy lies in breaking the vicious circle and restoring the confidence of the European people in the economic future of their own countries and of Europe as a whole. . . .

It is logical that the United States should do whatever it is able to do to assist in the return of normal economic health in the world, without which there can be no political stability and no assured peace. Our policy is directed not against any country or doctrine but against hunger, poverty, desperation, and chaos.

The United States sent $13 billion worth of food and other aid to help rebuild Western Europe. Marshall's proposal was formally titled the European Recovery Program, but it is now usually called the Marshall Plan. Marshall was awarded the Nobel Peace Prize in 1953.

the first African-American secretary of state. Missions of the State Department include promoting U.S. views and interests abroad, making treaties and other agreements with foreign governments, helping U.S. citizens and businesses overseas, and cooperating with international organizations such as the United Nations.

The State Department is not the only federal agency with a voice in foreign policy. An independent agency, the U.S. Agency for International Development (USAID), works together with the State Department in supporting aid and development projects in about seventy-five countries. The Department of Defense has a major say on national security issues, as does the Central Intelligence

The U.S. and the UN

The United States was a founding member of the United Nations, which has its headquarters in New York City. The U.S. gives more money to the UN than any other country and has worked together with the UN to bring the benefits of peace and development to many parts of the world.

Nonetheless, the U.S. and the UN have not always seen eye-to-eye. From the mid-1980s through the late 1990s, the U.S. lagged far behind in paying its annual UN dues. In 2003, the U.S. and several other countries went to war against Iraq without the approval of the UN Security Council, causing great controversy within the UN.

Agency. Because foreign trade is key to the U.S. economy, and is so central to U.S. relations with other countries, the Office of the U.S. Trade Representative, which is within the Executive Office of the President, also weighs in on foreign policy.

▼ **National Security Adviser Condoleezza Rice briefs the media in 2002.**

Another influential voice in the White House is the National Security Council. Aside from the president and the vice president, the White House official who speaks with the most authority on foreign affairs is the president's national security adviser. An ambitious national security adviser with a high public profile can rival the secretary of state in worldwide power and influence.

DEPARTMENT OF DEFENSE

Of all the cabinet departments, the largest by far is the Department of Defense (DOD). In addition to more than 650,000 civilian employees, the DOD oversees the activities of nearly 1,400,000 men and women on active duty in the United States military, whose primary mission is to protect the security of the United States. These full-time members of the armed forces include about 480,000 people serving in the Army, 378,000 in the Navy, 173,000 in the

Marine Corps, and 354,000 in the Air Force.

The Department of War was created in 1789, and the Department of the Navy was established nine years later. The country's defense forces were reorganized into the DOD in the late 1940s. The highest-ranking civilian in the DOD is the secretary of defense, while the DOD's highest-ranking military employee is the chairman of the Joint Chiefs of Staff (JCS). The JCS also includes the commanding officers of the Army, Navy, Air Force, and Marines.

Intelligence Matters

The U.S. government spends billions of dollars gathering information about other countries and about possible threats to national security. Much of this information is collected and analyzed by the Central Intelligence Agency, which was created in 1947.

Some information comes from public sources and is made available to readers worldwide through the annual *World Factbook* and other reports. Other information is gathered secretly and shown only to top officials in the White House, Congress, and government departments that deal directly with national security matters. Secret information that comes from human sources—known as HUMINT—requires a network of secret agents or spies. **Signals intelligence**—called SIGINT—relies on spy satellites and other tools for electronic eavesdropping.

▲ A CIA spy mission went awry when a U-2 aircraft flown by Francis Gary Powers was shot down over the Soviet Union on May 1, 1960.

The CIA also takes part in secret, or covert, operations on foreign soil. After it was revealed that the CIA had plotted to kill foreign leaders, President Gerald Ford banned such activities in 1975. This order, as applied by later presidents, does not stop the CIA from carrying out military missions—for example, in Afghanistan and Iraq. The CIA also has the power to undertake overseas missions to kill known terrorists, such as the leaders of **Al Qaeda**, the group that attacked the United States on September 11, 2001 (see Chapter 7).

The National Security Agency, which is part of the Department of Defense (DOD), deals with two top-secret tasks. The first is collecting and analyzing signals intelligence from overseas. The second is protecting U.S. communications from being intercepted by foreign countries and groups. The Defense Intelligence Agency, which is also part of the DOD, deals specifically with other countries' military activities.

The need for millions of American troops during World War II and several other twentieth-century conflicts made large-scale use of the military draft unavoidable. With the withdrawal of U.S. forces from Vietnam in 1973, however, the draft came to an end. Today, the United States has an all-volunteer military. No one is forced to serve who does not wish to. All males, however, are still required to contact the Selective Service System when they reach their eighteenth birthdays.

▲ Donald Rumsfeld was secretary of defense when the U.S. went to war in Afghanistan in 2001 and Iraq in 2003.

▼ Levittown, New York, and other sprawling suburban developments sprang up in the late 1940s and early 1950s, providing inexpensive housing to World War II veterans and their families.

High school graduates who are at least seventeen years of age, are not married or pregnant, and have no children to support may apply to one of the nation's four armed forces academies. These are the U.S. Military Academy, at West Point, New York; the U.S. Naval Academy, at Annapolis, Maryland; the U.S. Air Force Academy, near Colorado Springs, Colorado; and the U.S. Coast Guard Academy, in New London, Connecticut.

DEPARTMENT OF VETERANS AFFAIRS

The federal government has long recognized the debt it owes to the men and women who risked their lives to defend the United States in wartime. The Veterans Administration, which was created in 1930, became the Department of Veterans Affairs (VA) in 1989.

The VA spends more than $50 billion each year to assist military veterans and the spouses, children, and parents of veterans who have died. Most of that money pays for health care, education, training, counseling, home loans, and burial grounds. The VA operates more than 160 hospitals, about 800 clinics, and over 130 nursing homes throughout the United States.

LAW ENFORCEMENT AND HOMELAND SECURITY

For most of the country's history, law enforcement has been the job of state, county, and local governments. In 2000, for example, the United States had more than 15,000 separate state, county, and local police agencies, with a combined total of nearly 950,000 full-time employees. Of the more than 1,300,000 people in prison, about 90 percent were being held in state prisons and only 10 percent in federal prisons.

In recent years, the federal government has stepped up its police and homeland security efforts. Between 1993 and 2000, the number of full-time federal law enforcement officers increased from about 69,000 to more than 88,000. This increase has quickened since the terrorist attacks of 2001.

DEPARTMENT OF JUSTICE

The first attorney general of the United States, Edmund Randolph of Virginia, was appointed by President George Washington on September 26, 1789. His job was to give advice to the president on legal matters and to represent the United States in lawsuits brought before the Supreme Court. When he took up his duties as attorney general, Randolph had no department and no staff—not even a desk. Because Congress thought the federal workload would be light, Randolph was expected to keep his private law practice.

▲ The most important job of the Secret Service is to protect the president and other U.S. government leaders. This photo, taken in 1981, shows a Secret Service agent brandishing a submachine gun while other agents and police overcome the gunman who shot President Reagan.

▲ **Trainees take shotgun practice at the FBI Academy in Quantico, Virginia.**

Congress did not get around to creating a department for the attorney general until 1870, when the Department of Justice was established. Since then, as the size and scope of the federal government have expanded, so too have the laws the attorney general is expected to enforce. Major divisions of the Justice Department include the Federal Bureau of Prisons, which runs the federal prison system, and the Drug Enforcement Administration (DEA), which enforces federal laws against drug trafficking.

The Justice Department's most famous division is the Federal Bureau of Investigation (FBI). Founded in 1908, the FBI has more than 11,000 special agents and maintains offices throughout the United States and in many foreign countries. Although the FBI is best known for its "Ten Most Wanted" list, it actually enforces more than 200 federal laws and investigates thousands of cases. At the request of Congress, the White House, and other federal agencies, the FBI conducts background checks on people who are being considered for government jobs.

The "Drug Czar"

Within the Executive Office of the President is another antidrug agency—the Office of National Drug Control Policy. The director of this office is sometimes called the nation's "drug czar."

The job of the drug czar is to create a national strategy for the nation's drug control program. This strategy includes encouraging parents to talk with their children about drug abuse and producing a series of TV ads aimed at persuading young people not to use marijuana and other illegal drugs.

▲ **Members of the U.S. Customs Service and the Coast Guard inspect about two tons of marijuana seized from drug smugglers.**

Keeping an Eye on the FBI

From the late 1920s through the 1950s, no federal agency got better press coverage than the FBI. J. Edgar Hoover, the bureau's longtime director, had a genius for getting reporters to cover the FBI's successes in catching bank robbers, gangsters, and other criminals.

Since Hoover's death in 1972, however, a more balanced picture of the FBI has emerged. In addition to combating serious national security threats, the Hoover-era FBI targeted lawful antiwar and civil rights protests. Hoover kept secret files on many prominent Americans, including Martin Luther King, Jr. Hoover used these files to embarrass his political opponents and to increase his own power.

⏶ **A violent end to the Waco standoff led to a firestorm of criticism for the FBI and other federal agencies.**

More recently, the FBI and other federal law-enforcement officials were criticized for bungling an armed standoff in Waco, Texas. Federal agents stormed the Waco settlement of the Branch Davidian religious cult in April 1993, after a siege of fifty-one days. The armored assault—and the raging fire that followed—killed seventy-six cult members, including twenty-one children.

Critics have also charged that the FBI and other federal agencies in 2001 failed to heed important clues that Al Qaeda terrorists were planning to use hijacked aircraft as weapons against the United States.

Today, the FBI's highest priorities are to protect the nation against terrorism, spying by foreign countries, and computer-related crimes. The bureau maintains a huge collection of fingerprints, and exchanges fingerprint identification data with police agencies throughout the world. The FBI Laboratory is a world leader in the use of scientific methods to solve crimes.

A NATION AT WAR

Many Americans were shocked on September 11, 2001, when Al Qaeda terrorists crashed hijacked aircraft into the World Trade Center, destroying the Twin Towers, and into the Pentagon, the headquarters of the Department of Defense; a fourth aircraft went down in a field in

Pennsylvania. The attacks killed more than 3,000 people.

One month later, President George W. Bush launched Operation Enduring Freedom—a war in Afghanistan, where Al Qaeda had its headquarters. In March 2003, the United States went to war again. This war was called Operation Iraqi Freedom. By mid-April the United States and its allies had defeated the Iraqi government of Saddam Hussein. Bush argued that this war was necessary because if Hussein had been allowed to remain in power, he might have given terrorists chemical, biological, or nuclear weapons to use against the United States.

The September 11 attacks also led to the biggest reorganization of the U.S. government in more than fifty years. Changes included the creation of a new cabinet department—the Department of Homeland Security.

DEPARTMENT OF HOMELAND SECURITY

President Bush proposed the creation of the fifteenth cabinet department in a speech to the nation in June 2002. In that speech, he outlined the main responsibilities of the new department:

▼ Tom Ridge (right) became the nation's first secretary of homeland security in 2003.

The Department of Homeland Security will be charged with four primary tasks. This new agency will control our borders and prevent terrorists and explosives from entering our country. It will work with state and local authorities to respond quickly and effectively to emergencies. It will bring together our best scientists to develop technologies that detect biological, chemical, and nuclear weapons, and to discover the drugs and treatments to best protect our citizens. And this new department will review intelligence and law enforcement information from all agencies of government, and produce a single daily picture of threats against our homeland. Analysts will be responsible for imagining the worst, and planning to counter it.

The law creating the Department of Homeland Security was passed by Congress in November 2002. Tom Ridge, a former governor of Pennsylvania, was confirmed as the nation's first secretary of homeland security the following January. The department's major divisions include:

• **Secret Service:** Protects the president and other government leaders. Transferred from the Treasury Department.

• **U.S. Coast Guard:** Arrests drug smugglers, helps people and vessels in distress, and protects U.S. ports and waterways against terrorist attack, among other responsibilities. Transferred from the Department of Transportation. In wartime, Coast Guard vessels serve as part of the Navy.

• **Transportation Security Administration:** Conducts airport passenger and baggage screening. Transferred from the Department of Transportation.

• **Federal Emergency Management Agency (FEMA):** Assists local communities in responding to and recovering from earthquakes, hurricanes, tornadoes, floods, acts of terrorism, and other major disasters of all types. Formerly an independent agency.

The task of merging nearly two dozen separate agencies into an effective, unified department is expected to take many months, if not years.

FOIA— Your Right to Know

FOIA is not a government agency, but it has done a great deal to make government agencies more open. FOIA stands for Freedom of Information Act. This law, passed in 1966, gives people the right to obtain official government documents dealing with public health, product safety, and many other important subjects.

Another law, the Privacy Act of 1974, gives you the right to inspect certain files the government may have about you and to correct inaccurate information in those files.

▼ **FEMA helps towns and cities respond to natural disasters such as Hurricane Andrew, which devastated Homestead, Florida, in 1992.**

UNITED STATES CABINET DEPARTMENTS

The following table lists the cabinet departments in alphabetical order. The date following the name represents the year the department was established by Congress.

Department of Agriculture (1862)
http://www.usda.gov

Department of Commerce (1913)
http://www.commerce.gov

Department of Defense (1949)
http://www.defenselink.mil

Department of Education (1979)
http://www.ed.gov

Department of Energy (1977)
http://www.energy.gov

Department of Health and Human Services (1979)
http://www.os.dhhs.gov

Department of Homeland Security (2002)
http://www.dhs.gov/dhspublic

Department of Housing and Urban Development (1965)
http://www.hud.gov

Department of the Interior (1849)
http://www.doi.gov

Department of Justice (1870)
http://www.usdoj.gov

Department of Labor (1913)
http://www.dol.gov

Department of State (1789)
http://www.state.gov

Department of Transportation (1966)
http://www.dot.gov

Department of the Treasury (1789)
http://www.ustreas.gov

Department of Veterans Affairs (1989)
http://www.va.gov

NOTABLE CIVILIAN AGENCIES WITHIN THE EXECUTIVE BRANCH

Listed in alphabetical order. Independent agencies are indicated by an asterisk (*).

EXECUTIVE OFFICE OF THE PRESIDENT

Council of Economic Advisers
http://www.whitehouse.gov/cea/index.html

Council on Environmental Quality
http://www.whitehouse.gov/ceq/index.html

National Security Council
http://www.whitehouse.gov/nsc

Office of Management and Budget
http://www.whitehouse.gov/omb

Office of National Drug Control Policy
http://www.whitehousedrugpolicy.gov

Office of Science and Technology Policy
http://www.ostp.gov

Office of the U.S. Trade Representative
http://www.ustr.gov

OTHER EXECUTIVE BRANCH AGENCIES

Bureau of Alcohol, Tobacco, Firearms and Explosives
http://www.atf.gov
Cabinet Dept.: Justice

Bureau of the Census
http://www.census.gov
Cabinet Dept.: Interior

Bureau of Indian Affairs
http://www.doi.gov/bureau-indian-affairs.html
Cabinet Dept.: Interior

Centers for Disease Control and Prevention
http://www.cdc.gov
Cabinet Dept.: Health and Human Services

Centers for Medicare and Medicaid Services
http://cms.hhs.gov
Cabinet Dept.: Health and Human Services

*Central Intelligence Agency
http://www.odci.gov

*Commission on Civil Rights
http://www.usccr.gov

*Consumer Product Safety Commission
http://www.cpsc.gov

Drug Enforcement Administration
http://www.dea.gov
Cabinet Dept.: Justice

*Environmental Protection Agency
http://www.epa.gov

*Equal Employment Opportunity Commission
http://www.eeoc.gov

Federal Aviation Administration
http://www2.faa.gov
Cabinet Dept.: Transportation

Federal Bureau of Investigation
http://www.fbi.gov
Cabinet Dept.: Justice

NOTABLE CIVILIAN AGENCIES WITHIN THE EXECUTIVE BRANCH

Listed in alphabetical order. Independent agencies are indicated by an asterisk (*).

Federal Bureau of Prisons
http://www.bop.gov
Cabinet Dept.: Justice

*Federal Communications Commission
http://www.fcc.gov

*Federal Deposit Insurance Corporation
http://www.fdic.gov

*Federal Election Commission
http://www.fec.gov

Federal Emergency Management Agency
http://www.fema.gov
Cabinet Dept.: Homeland Security

Federal Highway Administration
http://www.fhwa.dot.gov
Cabinet Dept.: Transportation

*Federal Reserve System
http://www.federalreserve.gov

*Federal Trade Commission
http://www.ftc.gov

Fish and Wildlife Service
http://www.fws.gov
Cabinet Dept.: Interior

Food and Drug Administration
http://www.fda.gov
Cabinet Dept.: Health and Human Services

Food and Nutrition Service
http://www.fns.usda.gov/fns
Cabinet Dept.: Agriculture

Forest Service
http://www.fs.fed.us
Cabinet Dept.: Agriculture

*General Services Administration
http://www.gsa.gov

Internal Revenue Service
http://www.irs.gov
Cabinet Dept.: Treasury

*National Aeronautics and Space Administration
http://www.nasa.gov

*National Archives and Records Administration
http://www.archives.gov

*National Endowment for the Arts
http://www.arts.gov

*National Endowment for the Humanities
http://www.neh.fed.us

National Institutes of Health
http://www.nih.gov
Cabinet Dept.: Health and Human Services

National Oceanic and Atmospheric Administration
http://www.noaa.gov
Cabinet Dept.: Commerce

National Park Service
http://www.nps.gov
Cabinet Dept.: Interior

*National Railroad Passenger Corp. (Amtrak)
http://www.amtrak.com

*National Science Foundation
http://www.nsf.gov

National Security Agency
http://www.nsa.gov
Cabinet Dept.: Defense

*National Transportation Safety Board
http://www.ntsb.gov

*Nuclear Regulatory Commission
http://www.nrc.gov

National Weather Service
http://www.nws.noaa.gov
Cabinet Dept.: Commerce

Occupational Safety and Health Administration
http://www.osha.gov
Cabinet Dept.: Labor

*Office of Personnel Management
http://www.opm.gov

Office of the Surgeon General
http://www.surgeongeneral.gov/sgoffice.htm
Cabinet Dept.: Health and Human Services

*Peace Corps
http://www.peacecorps.gov

*Securities and Exchange Commission
http://www.sec.gov

*Selective Service System
http://www.sss.gov

*Social Security Administration
http://www.ssa.gov

Surgeon General
http://www.surgeongeneral.gov
Cabinet Dept.: Health and Human Services

Transportation Security Administration
http://www.tsa.gov/public
Cabinet Dept.: Homeland Security

U.S. Mint
http://www.usmint.gov
Cabinet Dept.: Treasury

*U.S. Postal Service
http://www.usps.com

U.S. Secret Service
http://www.secretservice.gov/index.shtml
Cabinet Dept.: Homeland Security

TIME LINE

1789	Constitution comes into effect. George Washington takes office as first president of the United States. Departments of State, Treasury, and War established. First attorney general and postmaster general appointed.
1849	Department of the Interior established.
1862	Department of Agriculture created.
1870	Department of Justice established.
1908	Federal Bureau of Investigation (FBI) established.
1913	Separate departments of Commerce and Labor established.
1935	Congress passes Social Security Act.
1947	Central Intelligence Agency (CIA) established.
1949	Department of Defense established.
1958	National Aeronautics and Space Administration (NASA) created.
1965	Department of Housing and Urban Development established.
1966	Department of Transportation established.
1970	Environmental Protection Agency created. U.S. Postal Service becomes independent agency.
1977	Department of Energy established.
1979	Department of Health, Education, and Welfare (created 1953) becomes Department of Health and Human Services. Separate Department of Education established.
1989	Veterans Administration (established 1930) becomes Department of Veterans Affairs.
2002	Department of Homeland Security established.

GLOSSARY

Al Qaeda: group that masterminded the terrorist attack against the United States on September 11, 2001.

ambassadors: officials who represent the United States in foreign countries.

attorney general: the head of the Department of Justice.

cabinet: the heads of the major federal government departments.

civilians: people who are not members of the armed forces.

Civil War: a war (1861–65) between northern and southern states that began when the South (Confederacy) rebelled against the Union. Slavery in the South was a major cause of the conflict, which was won by the North.

conservative: favoring traditional views and values, while seeking to slow the pace of social change.

czar: someone who holds great power or authority.

endangered species: a plant or animal that is at risk of becoming extinct.

executive branch: the part of the United States government headed by the president.

federal government: the government of the United States.

fossil fuels: energy sources such as oil, coal, and natural gas, formed from the remains of prehistoric plant and animal life.

framers: a name for the group of political leaders who wrote the Constitution.

global warming: a steady increase in the temperature of Earth's atmosphere, changing the climate in ways that threaten the environment.

impeachment: the power of Congress to remove the president. The House of Representatives impeaches the president by bringing charges against him, but he cannot be removed from office unless tried and convicted by the Senate.

regulatory agency: a government body that issues and enforces rules limiting how private firms may act.

signals intelligence: data gathered by spy satellites and other electronic eavesdropping devices.

World War II: world conflict fought between 1939 and 1945. The Allies (including the United States, the Soviet Union, Britain, and France) defeated the Axis powers (Germany, Italy, and Japan).

TO FIND OUT MORE

BOOKS

Grossman, Mark.
Encyclopedia of the United States Cabinet.
Santa Barbara, CA: ABC-CLIO, 2000.

Kramer, Barbara.
Madeleine Albright: First Woman Secretary of State.
Springfield, NJ: Enslow, 2000.

Remy, Richard C.
United States Government: Democracy in Action.
New York: Glencoe-McGraw-Hill, 2000.

Richie, Jason.
Secretaries of State: Making Foreign Policy.
Minneapolis: Oliver Press, 2002.

Richie, Jason.
Secretaries of War, Navy, and Defense: Ensuring National Security.
Minneapolis: Oliver Press, 2002.

Sanford, William R., and Carl R. Green.
Basic Principles of American Government.
New York: Amsco, 1997 (2nd ed.).

INTERNET SITES

The Cabinet
http://www.whitehouse.gov/government/cabinet.html
Shows all top cabinet officials.

The Executive Office of the President
http://www.whitehouse.gov/government/eop.html
Links to many agencies that are part of the Executive Office of the President.

Federal Citizen Information Center
http://www.pueblo.gsa.gov/
Consumer news and information.

FedStats
http://www.fedstats.gov/
Gateway to U.S. government statistics and web sites of many federal agencies.

FirstGov
http://www.firstgov.gov/Agencies/Federal/Executive.shtml
Links to all offices of the executive branch.

INDEX

Page numbers in *italic* type refer to illustration captions.

INDEX (CONT.)